Earthquakes, Eruptions, and Other Events that Change Earth

Natalie Hyde

 Crabtree Publishing Company
www.crabtreebooks.com

Author
Natalie Hyde

Publishing plan research and development
Reagan Miller

Editor
Crystal Sikkens

Proofreader and indexer
Wendy Scavuzzo

Design
Samara Parent

Photo research
Tammy McGarr

Prepress technician
Tammy McGarr

Print and production coordinator
Margaret Amy Salter

Photographs
iStock: title page © BluesandViews; p17 © winhorse
Shutterstock: p5 © think4photop; p11 © Somjin Klong-ugkara;
p19 © My Good Images
Superstock: p22 Ragnar Th. Sigurdsson / age fotostock
Thinkstock: p9
Wikimedia Commons: p12 Jay Robinson/NPS; p16 David Rydevik

All other images from Shutterstock

Library and Archives Canada Cataloguing in Publication

Hyde, Natalie, 1963-, author
    Earthquakes, eruptions, and other events that change Earth / Natalie Hyde.

(Earth's processes close-up)
Includes index.
Issued in print and electronic formats.
ISBN 978-0-7787-1725-6 (bound).--ISBN 978-0-7787-1772-0 (paperback).--
ISBN 978-1-4271-1609-3 (pdf).--ISBN 978-1-4271-1605-5 (html)

    1. Earthquakes--Juvenile literature. 2. Volcanoes--Juvenile literature.
I. Title.

QE521.3.H94 2015   j551.2   C2015-903925-8
                                          C2015-903926-6

Library of Congress Cataloging-in-Publication Data

Hyde, Natalie, 1963-
  Earthquakes, eruptions, and other events that change Earth / Natalie Hyde.
    pages cm. -- (Earth's processes close-up)
  Includes index.
  ISBN 978-0-7787-1725-6 (reinforced library binding) --
ISBN 978-0-7787-1772-0 (pbk.) --
ISBN 978-1-4271-1609-3 (electronic pdf) --
ISBN 978-1-4271-1605-5 (electronic html)
  1. Earth (Planet)--Surface--Juvenile literature. 2. Earthquakes--Juvenile
literature. 3. Volcanoes--Juvenile literature. I. Title.
  QE511.H84 2016
  551.2--dc23
                                  2015024022

Crabtree Publishing Company

www.crabtreebooks.com   1-800-387-7650

Printed in Canada/102015/IH20150821

Published in Canada
Crabtree Publishing
616 Welland Ave.
St. Catharines, Ontario
L2M 5V6

Published in the United States
Crabtree Publishing
PMB 59051
350 Fifth Avenue, 59th Floor
New York, New York 10118

Published in the United Kingdom
Crabtree Publishing
Maritime House
Basin Road North, Hove
BN41 1WR

Published in Australia
Crabtree Publishing
3 Charles Street
Coburg North
VIC 3058

Contents

Planet of change

Earth's surface is always changing. Most of these changes happen slowly. They can take hundreds or even thousands of years. Some changes, however, happen quickly. In fact, Earth's surface can change in a matter of minutes, hours, or days.

The movement of water causes changes to rocks on the coast.

Big changes

Natural disasters, such as earthquakes, volcanoes, and **tsunamis**, can happen without warning. They can change Earth's surface in a big way very quickly. An earthquake's shaking can create large holes or cracks in the land. A volcano's hot **lava** can create new landforms when cooled. The wall of water from a tsunami can destroy forests, roads, and buildings.

Which is more dangerous— slow changes to Earth's surface or quick changes? Why?

Natural disasters can be very dangerous for people and animals.

5

Layers

Earth is not a solid ball. If you were to cut our planet open, you would see it is made up of four layers.

The inner core is at the center. It is a solid ball of metal. Around this inner core is the outer core. This layer is liquid metal. The next layer is called the mantle. The mantle is made of solid rock and minerals. The top layer is the crust.

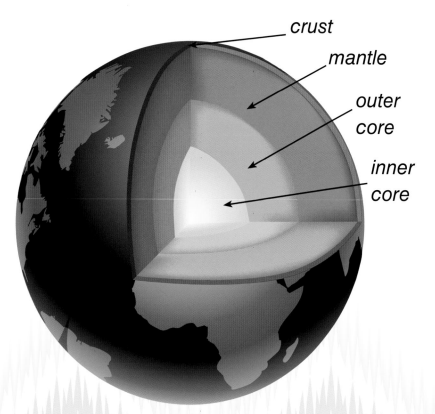

crust

mantle

outer core

inner core

Rocky crust

The crust is the thinnest layer. It is made of rock. This is the layer that we live on. The rocks and minerals in the crust are shaped into landforms. Low landforms fill with water to make lakes, rivers, and oceans. Earth's **processes** are always at work changing the crust.

Cliffs, hills, and mountains are raised landforms.

Earthquakes

Earth's crust is divided into plates. A plate is a huge sheet of rock. The plates fit together like big puzzle pieces to form the surface. The plates are moving and rubbing against each other very slowly. Sometimes the edge of one plate is pushed under another plate. This causes an earthquake. During an earthquake, the ground shakes suddenly.

Earth's crust is made up of a few large plates and many smaller plates.

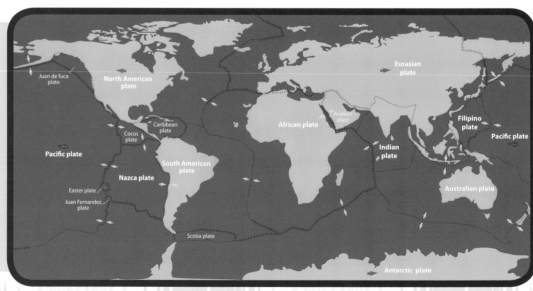

Juan de fuca plate
North American plate
Eurasian plate
Caribbean plate
Arabian plate
African plate
Filipino plate
Pacific plate
Cocos plate
Indian plate
Pacific plate
South American plate
Nazca plate
Easter plate
Juan Fernandez plate
Australian plate
Scotia plate
Antarctic plate

Earth's plates can also push together and can cause the rock to bend and fold. This process can create mountains.

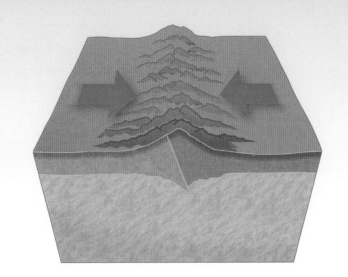

Moving and shaking

Earthquakes happen around the world every day. Most are not strong enough to cause any damage. Some, however, can cause the ground to shake violently. During these strong earthquakes, buildings can crumble and fall, and roads can crack and split.

What changes on Earth's surface can we see that are caused by the movement of Earth's plates?

Landslides

During a landslide, rocks and soil suddenly break loose and slide down hills or mountains. Landslides can happen for different reasons. Rivers can eat away at the base of hills and mountains, causing the **earth** above to fall. Heavy rains can also cause landslides when wet soil turns to mud. The slippery mud will then move downhill quickly.

Earthquakes can shake rocks and soil loose and cause a landslide.

Slipping and sliding

Landslides can be as small as a few large rocks rolling down a hill. They can also be as large as the whole side of a mountain sliding away. The biggest landslides can move a lot of ground very quickly. They change the shape and size of landforms. They fill valleys with soil and rocks. Landslides can happen underwater, too.

Dirt and rocks in landslides can move as fast as a car on city streets.

Volcanoes

A volcano is an opening in Earth's crust where hot, melted rock and **ash** from inside Earth erupts, or shoots out. Some eruptions happen once every few years and last only a couple of hours. Other volcanoes continue erupting for weeks, months, or even years.

The Kīlauea Volcano in Hawaii has been erupting since 1983.

Melting rocks

Volcanoes reshape Earth's surface. When the lava shoots out of the volcano, it flows down the sides and over the land below. The lava is so hot that it can melt rock. Boulders and hills can melt away. When the lava cools, it hardens into new rock. This new rock is full of minerals. After a few years, the new rock breaks down and turns into rich farmland.

A large, flat area of cooled lava is called a lava field.

Volcanic islands

Volcanoes can create new islands. When a volcano erupts, lava flows out of it. Some volcanoes erupt underwater. As they erupt over and over, the lava cools and builds up a cone-shaped mountain around the opening. When the mountain gets big enough it breaks through the surface of the water, creating an island.

The Stromboli Volcano has been erupting for at least 2,000 years.

Making islands

The Hawaiian Islands are volcanic islands found in the Pacific Ocean. The islands are the **peaks** of large mountains formed under the ocean by volcanic eruptions. Some Hawaiian Island volcanoes are no longer erupting. Others are still **active** and creating new land.

How can volcanoes destroy land, but also create new land?

Tsunamis

A tsunami can be as high as 115 feet (35 m). That is as tall as a ten-story building!

A tsunami is a giant wave. Tsunamis are caused by changes in the ocean floor. Underwater earthquakes, landslides, and volcanic eruptions can all cause tsunamis. The **force** from these natural disasters can make the water rise. This will start a wave that speeds through the water until it reaches land.

Wall of water

A tsunami is one of the most damaging forces on Earth. It can race toward land as fast as a jet plane. It can wipe out villages, and even islands. It can move soil and rocks as much as 620 miles (1,000 km).

Tsunamis are strong enough to move huge ships onto land.

Building up and tearing down

Earth's processes can build up and tear down landforms. Landslides change the shape of hills and mountains. Tsunamis eat away at the land along the coast. Volcanoes build up Earth's surface and earthquakes tear it down.

The island of Iceland is growing larger each year. It has many active volcanoes. The lava from these volcanoes creates new land.

In 2015, a strong earthquake shook the country of Nepal. The shaking tore down buildings and destroyed roads. Rocks and soil buried villages.

Our changing Earth

These changes can **threaten** the lives of people, plants, and animals. But, they are also a chance for new life to grow. New landforms become homes for plants and animals. New mineral-rich soil produces food to feed people around the world.

Shake it up!

This activity will show you how earthquakes change landforms.

You will need:

extra soil or sand

water

shallow pan with a thick layer of soil or sand

Steps

1. Place the shallow pan with soil on the table.

2. Wet the extra soil or sand with water until just damp.

3. Using the damp soil, form mountains and hills of different sizes and shapes. Put them on top of the layer of soil in the pan.

4. Shake the box to simulate an earthquake.

Asking questions

- What happened to the mountains and hills you made during your earthquake?

- Which mountain gets damaged more: a tall and narrow mountain, or a wide and flat mountain?

On the job

Scientists have a lot to learn about Earth's processes. Seismologists are people who study earthquakes. They want to learn when and where earthquakes will happen. Volcanologists are people who study volcanoes. They are looking for signs of a coming eruption. They study the buildup of pressure under the ground.

Discovering new information about natural disasters can help save people's lives.

Learning more

Books

Everything Volcanoes and Earthquakes by Kathy Furgang,
National Geographic Children's Books, 2013.

*Magic Tree House Fact Tracker #15: Tsunamis and Other
Natural Disasters* by Mary Pope Osborne,
Random House Books for Young Readers, 2007.

Volcanoes on Earth by Bobbie Kalman,
Crabtree Publishing Company, 2008.

Websites

The Mountain Environment investigates volcanoes:
**http://resources.woodlands-junior.kent.sch.uk/homework/
mountains/volcanoeruptions.html**

Fun facts, puzzles, and games about earthquakes from the U.S.
Geological Survey: **http://earthquake.usgs.gov/learn/kids/**

The Geography for Kids site explains tsunamis:
http://www.kidsgeo.com/geography-for-kids/0146B-tsunamis.php

Words to know

active (AK-tiv) adjective In motion

ash (ash) noun A powder that is left after something burns

earth (urth) noun Soil and dirt

force (fohrs) noun The strength or energy of something

lava (LAV-uh) noun Melted rock that flows out of a volcano

natural disaster (NACH-er-uhl dih-ZAH-ster) noun An event that causes great damage

peak (peek) noun The pointed top of a mountain

processes (PROH-ses-es) noun Actions or steps

threaten (THRET-n) verb To put at risk

tsunami (tsoo-NAH-mee) noun A huge wave caused by an earthquake underwater

A noun is a person, place, or thing.

An adjective is a word that tells you what something is like.

A verb is an action word that tells you what someone or something does.

Index